Based on
alphabet designs
by Becky Higgins

AmericanGirl

Published by Pleasant Company Publications

Original Alphabet Art Copyright © Becky Higgins

Illustrations and Text Copyright © 2001 by Pleasant Company

Visit our Web site: americangirl.com

Printed in Hong Kong

02 03 04 05 06 07 08 C&C 10 9 8 7 6 5

American Girl Library® and the American Girl logo
are registered trademarks of Pleasant Company.

Editorial Development: Camela Decaire, Michelle Watkins.

Alphabet designs included in this book are based on designs previously published in *The Art of Creative Lettering*. Published by arrangement with Creating Keepsakes Books.

Art Direction: Chris Lorette David. Design: Camela Decaire.
Photography: Jamie Young. Stylists: Camela Decaire,
Tricia Doherty, Sarajane Lien, Laura Moberly.
Production: Lori Armstrong, Janette Sowinski.

Becky Higgins is a scrapbook artist and creative editor of *Creating Keepsakes* scrapbook magazine. She travels extensively throughout the United States to scrapbooking conventions, giving workshops on lettering and other scrapbook-related topics.

Library of Congress Cataloging-in-Publication Data

Letter art
p. cm
ISBN 1-58485-287-9
1. Lettering—Juvenile literature. [1. Lettering.]
NK3620 .L477 2001
745.6'1–dc21
00-059398

From  **to**

Turn the letters of the **alphabet**—and numbers, too!—into amazing works of art. It's easy. It just takes a little patience and a bit of imagination. This book will get you started with **step-by-step** lettering instructions, some great **alphabet ideas,** and lots of **tips** and tricks. There's a special section at the back to practice in and tracing paper to help you.

Use your new lettering skills on folders, cards, invitations, posters, school projects, and scrapbook pages—the **possibilities** are endless. So pick up a pencil, and let's letter!

Pencils

Sketching your letters in pencil first is a **MUST**. It lets you figure out **shapes** and fuss with patterns till you get them just right. Sketching will also help you adjust your letter and word **spacing**. Press lightly so that stray lines are easy to erase.

Rulers and Erasers

Use a ruler to draw **guidelines** at the top and the bottom of your letters so that they will stay even in height and **level** on your paper. Remember, there's nothing wrong with having to **erase**. You'll probably need to erase a lot. Use a good-quality eraser that won't damage your paper or smear your pencil lines.

SUPPLIES

for getting started

Coloring Tools

Experiment with a rainbow of paints, markers, pencils, crayons, and chalks when coloring your letters. Pens are perfect for outlining letters and drawing details. The finer the pen point, the more control you will have.

Tracing Paper

If you decide to try some of the fancier lettering styles, you may want to trace the letters onto tracing paper. To transfer the traced letters to paper, see page 9.

5

1. Sketch your basic letters in pencil. Then decide on a style. If you want, you can make just the vertical lines thicker, or you can outline the whole letter.

2. Add details and decorations to your letters. You can also add serifs, the small "feet" at the ends of some letters.

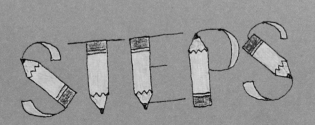

to lettering

3. Outline the details and decorations with a pen or thin marker. Black ink makes a clean edge, but you can also use colors. Next, outline the letters.

4. When all ink is dry, erase any leftover pencil lines. Then color in the letters and decorations. Try filling the spaces inside the letters with patterns. See the ideas on pages 10 and 11!

to a project

Every lettering project follows the same basic steps. Start by sketching out a few designs on scrap paper. When you have one that you like, plan its actual size. Using a ruler, mark the size on tracing paper. Draw guidelines to help you place your letters, and then pencil in your final design. You'll probably need to erase a few times to get the sizing right, so draw lightly!

Letter guidelines

If you plan to have a border, be sure to mark out space for it.

Marking the center helps you position your art.

Use a pencil to draw over the exact lines of your drawing, then remove the drawing. The pencil lead you rubbed on the back of your drawing will leave a faint outline on your paper. Use it as a guide, and start coloring!

To transfer the drawing to your final project, rub pencil lead lightly across the back of the drawing.

Turn the drawing right-side up (shaded-side down) on top of your final piece. Position it carefully, and tape it in place.

IDEAS
to inspire you

By varying the colors and patterns you use to fill in your letters, you can create lots of different alphabets. Take off with these ideas! If you're making a poster or card, let the lettering be the center of attention, and choose any pattern you like. If you're putting together a scrapbook page, pick a pattern that suits your subject, and match colors to your photos. For example, a balloon pattern would go well with a birthday theme.

FLOWER GARDEN

It's an alphabet in bloom!

Mix and match flower styles! Use the samples
shown, or make up your own.

When,
April 9, 10 A.M.

Where
Alison's house
801 Elmwood Ave.

Bring a
basket!

Easter
Egg
Hunt

Add your own touch! Bugs,
butterflies, and animals
can boost the fun.

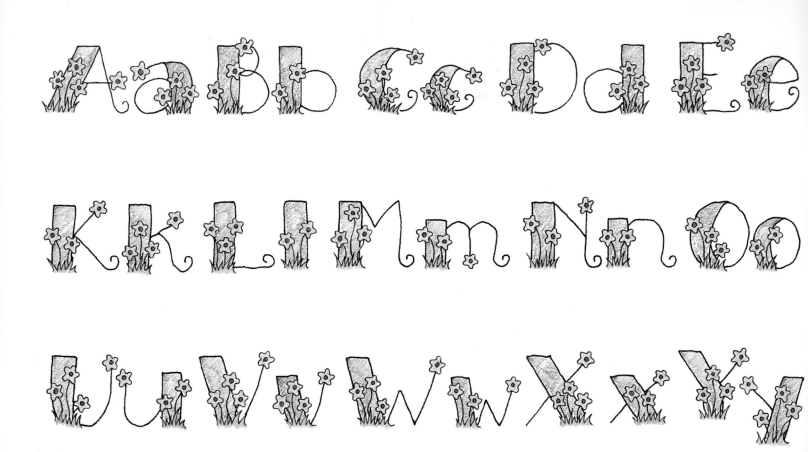

Flower Garden

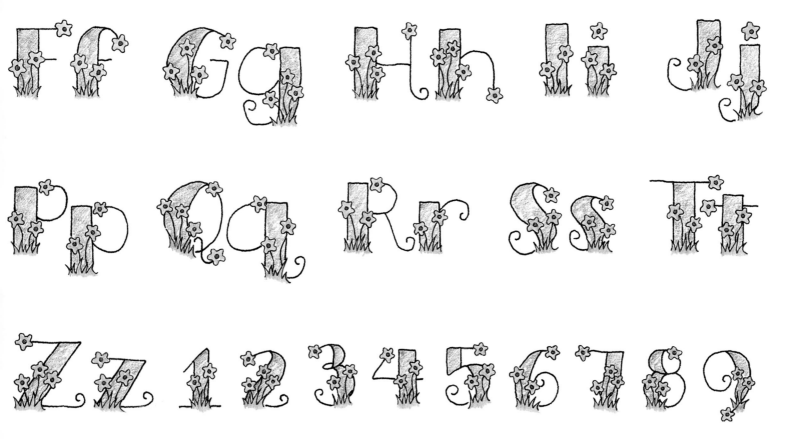

Flower Garden

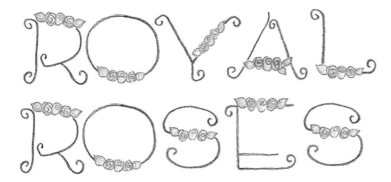

ROYAL ROSES

Use this delicate font for anything sweet.

Make these letters very wide so that you'll
have room for the roses.

These letters were drawn
with a special pen that
creates its own outline as
you write. You can find one
at your local craft store.

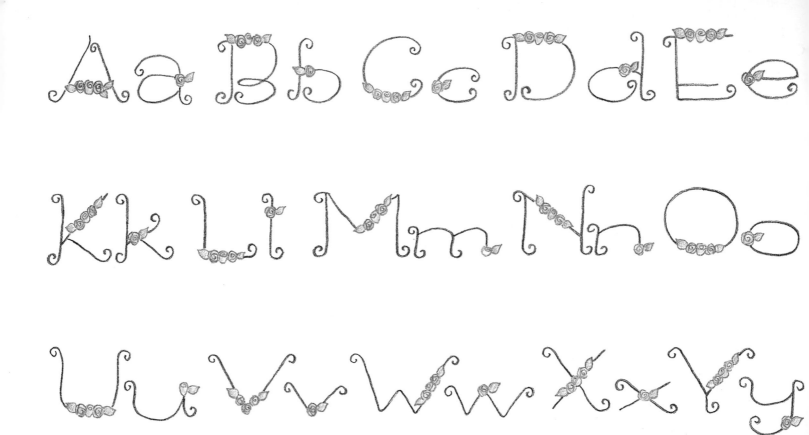

Royal Roses

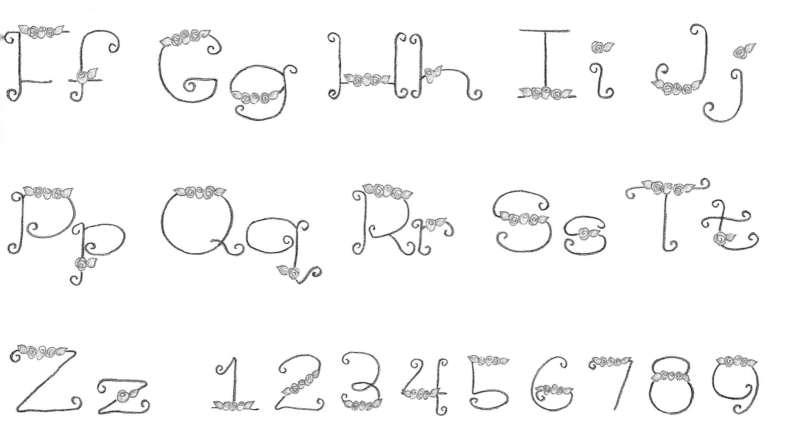

Royal Roses

HAPPY HEARTS

Show your true feelings!

Hang a heart from every horizontal letter line.

Outline the letters with
a contrasting color.
Make the hearts differ-
ent colors, too, or play
with the ribbons they
hang from.

Aa Bb Cc Dd Ee

Kk Ll Mm Nn Oo

Uu Vv Ww Xx Yy

Happy Hearts

Ff Gg Hh Ii Jj

Pp Qq Rr Ss Tt

Zz 1234567889

Happy Hearts

LOVELY LEAVES

Twining vines climb around these letters.

Color the vine and leaf lines first. Be careful not to cross
over them when you outline and color in the letter shape!

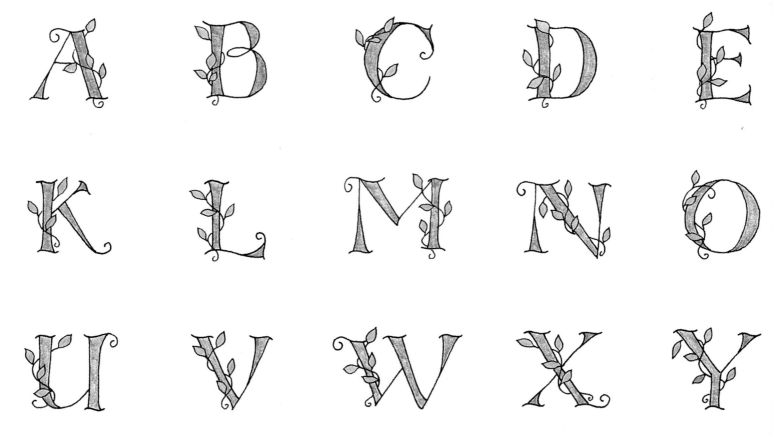

Lovely Leaves

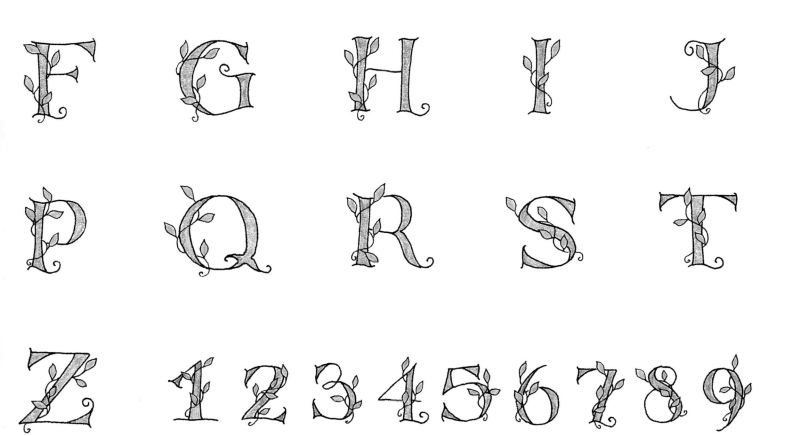

Lovely Leaves

Brighten any page with sunshine!

Instead of drawing the sun shapes, you can cut them from colored paper.

Try putting only the first letters of words in this style, or place whole words inside one box.

Summer Sunshine

F G H I J

P Q R S T

Z 1 2 3 4 5 6 7 8 9

Summer Sunshine

PENCIL POWER

Make your point with this sharp look!

On large letters, draw in vertical lines to show the
six-sided shape of a standard pencil.

DRAW • SKETCH

SCRIBBLE •

Show

SCHOOL

Try using crayons,
pens, or paintbrushes
in the letters instead
of pencils.

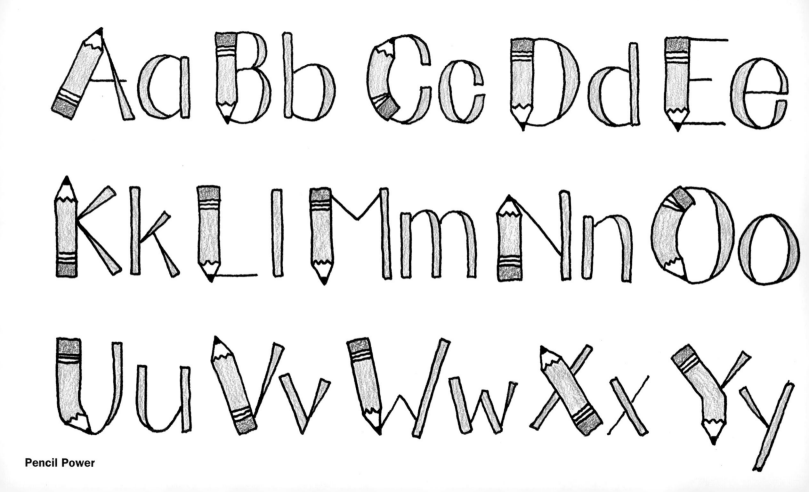

Pencil Power

Ff Gg Hh Ii Jj

Pp Qq Rr Ss Tt

Zz 1 2 3 4 5 6 7 8 9

Pencil Power

SUPER STACKS

Pile them high!

Keep the boxes slightly slanted and wobbly.

You can use fabric paint to create these alphabets, too. Here, tiny stacks look almost like beads.

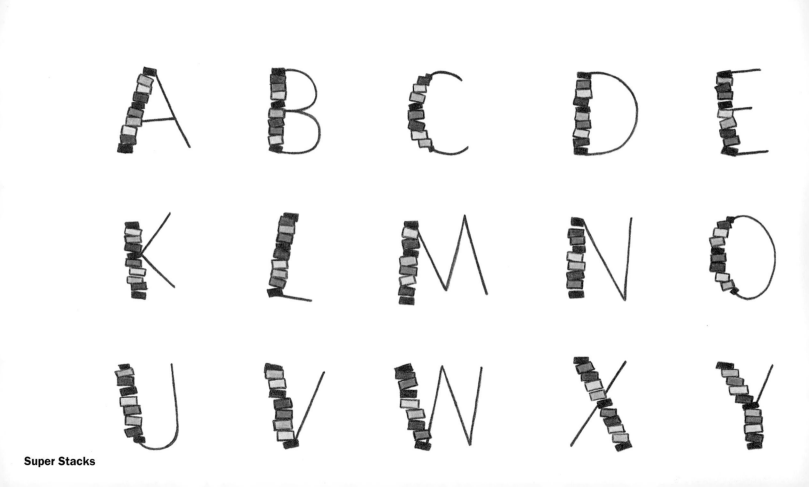

Super Stacks

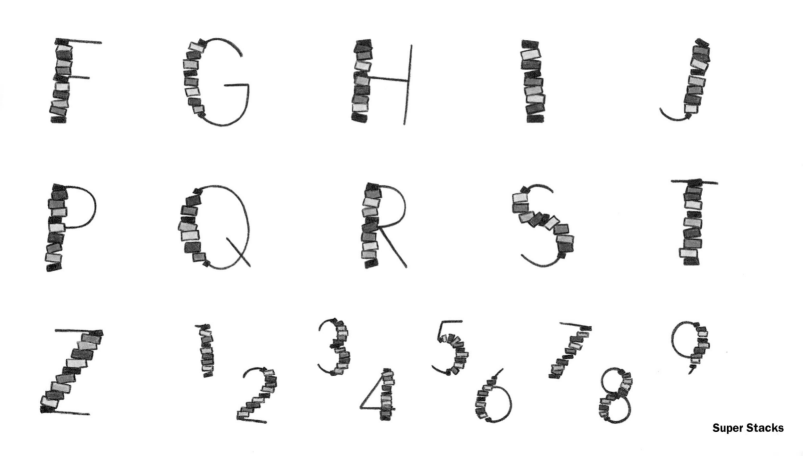

Super Stacks

TALL TREES

A natural favorite!

Each of these trees is simply a narrow triangle
on top of a small rectangular trunk.

Cut the trees out of paper for a textured look.

Tall Trees

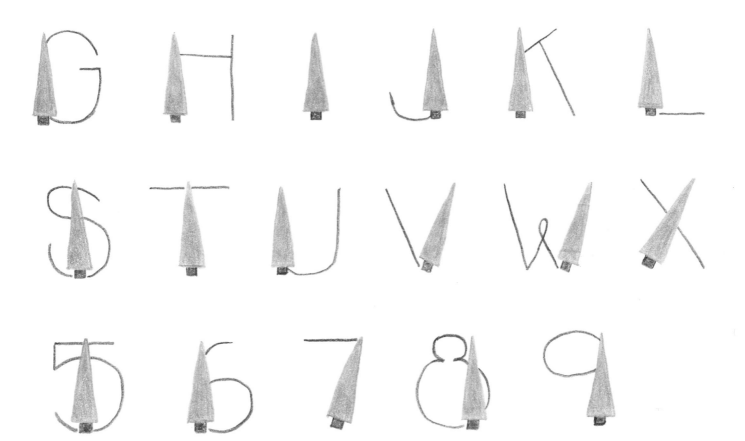

Tall Trees

BOUNCING BALLS

Put a spin on your signature!

 A tennis ball needs just one U-shaped curve.

 Mark one line across a basketball's center. Draw curved lines across it.

 Make the two lines of stitching on a baseball by drawing tiny Vs.

 Put hexagons in the center of a soccer ball.

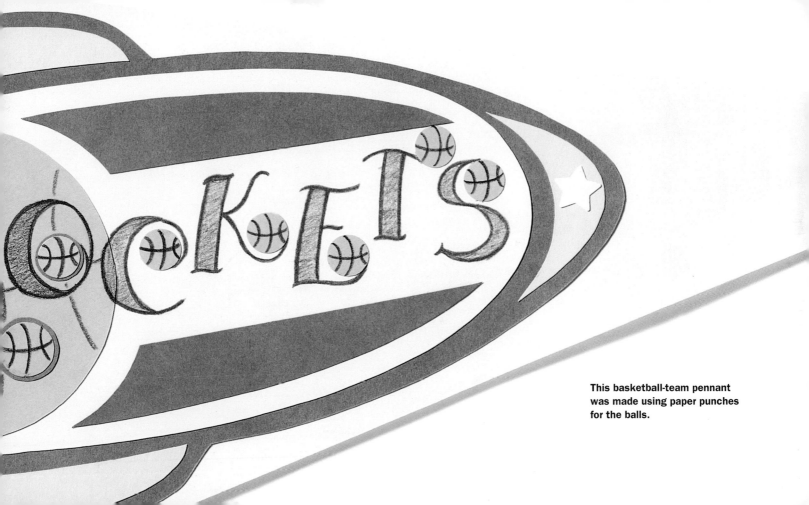

This basketball-team pennant
was made using paper punches
for the balls.

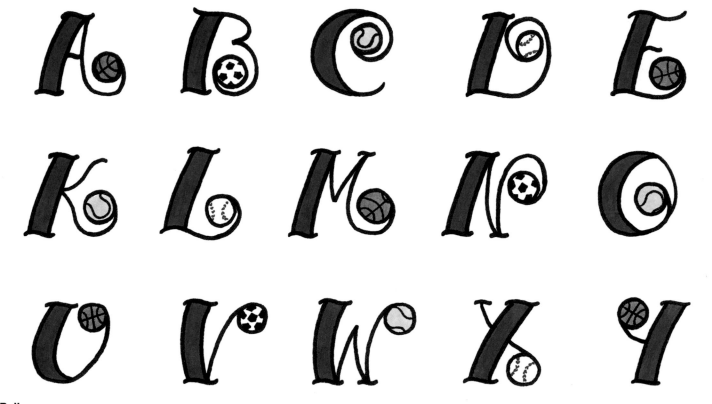

Bouncing Balls

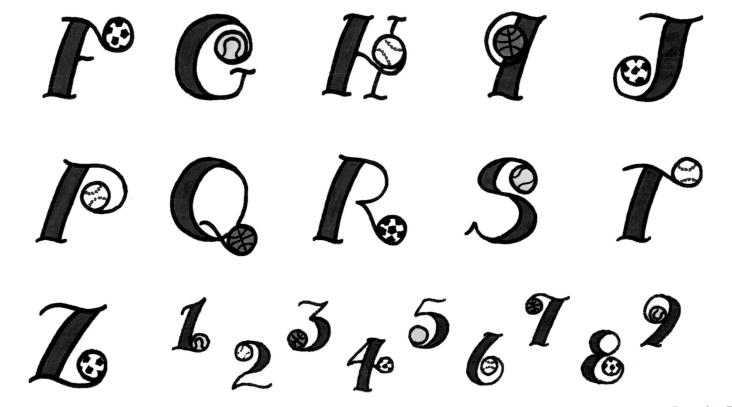

Bouncing Balls

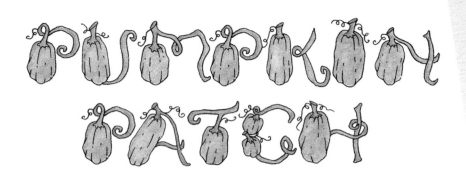

Fun for fall!

Slightly rounded lines inside the pumpkins give them a 3-D effect.

Add jack-o'-lantern faces for the perfect Halloween touch!

...or Treat!

It's a

R.S.V.P.
R.I.P.
5 – 2074

Haunting
Hallowe...
Party

Rachel's ho...
Friday, Octob...
7 – 9 PM

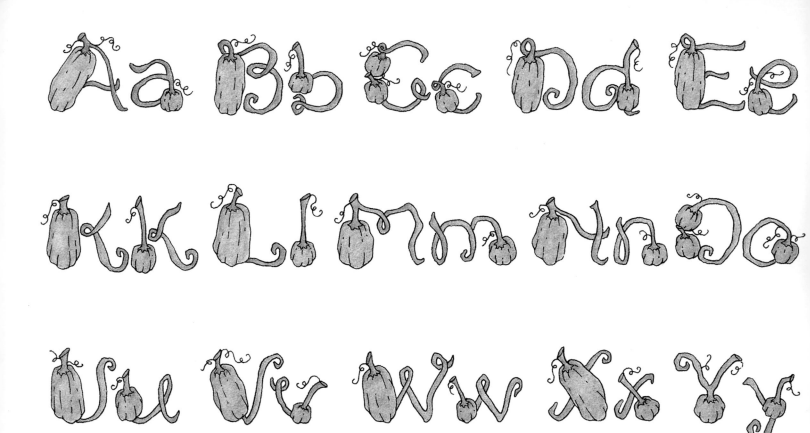

Pumpkin Patch

Pumpkin Patch

BRIGHT BOUQUETS

Pick a bouquet for spring, summer, or fall.

You can substitute just about anything for the flower bouquets in this alphabet, from bunches of balloons to sheaves of wheat.

Bright Bouquets

Bright Bouquets

WINTER SNOWCAPS

Frost the tops of letters with deep drifts.

Use a white gel pen to create the snowcaps
if you're using colored paper.

Winter Snowcaps

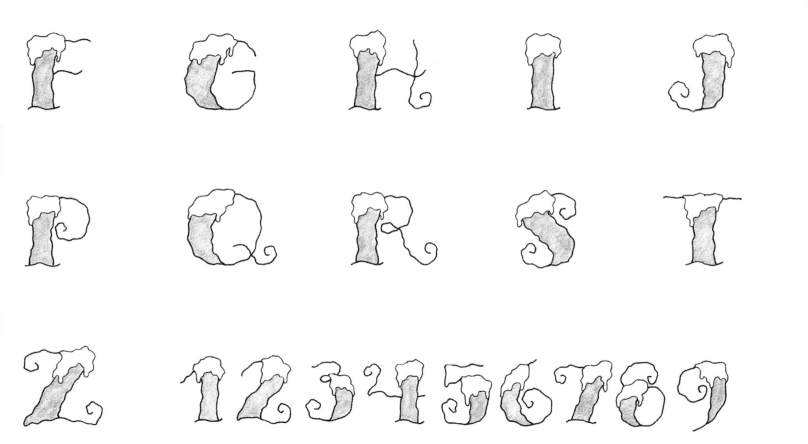

Winter Snowcaps

HOLIDAY HOLLY

An evergreen favorite!

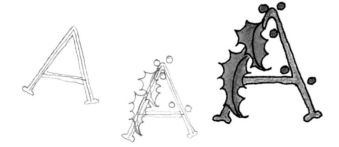

To make a holly leaf, draw two curvy, scalloped edges,
and connect them at each end.

Shhh!
Secret Santa
party
Where: Tara's House
When: 12:00 Noon
Saturday

Aa Bb Cc Dd Ee

Kk Ll Mm Nn Oo

Uu Vv Ww Xx Yy

Holiday Holly

Ff Gg Hh Ii Jj

Pp Qq Rr Ss Tt

Zz 1 2 3 4 5 6 7 8 9

Holiday Holly

Practice Pages

Use the alphabet **outlines** in this section to **try** out **color** combinations, test new **patterns,** add interesting **details,** and practice, practice, practice! The more letters you draw, the easier it will seem. And the more you **experiment,** the more unique your lettering style will become. Have **fun!**

Aa Bb Cc Dd Ee

Kk Ll Mm Nn Oo

Uu Vv Ww Xx Yy

Ff Gg Hh Ii Jj

Pp Qq Rr Ss Tt

Zz 1 2 3 4 5 6 7 8 9

Aa Bb Cc Dd Ee

Kk Ll Mm Nn Oo

Uu Vv Ww Xx Yy

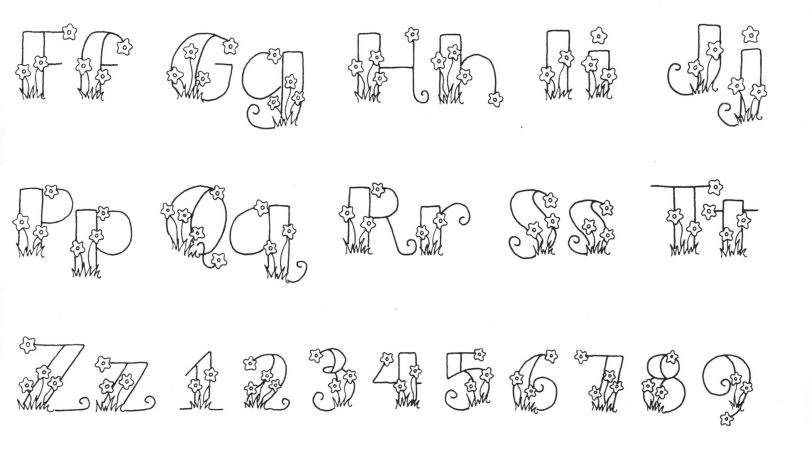

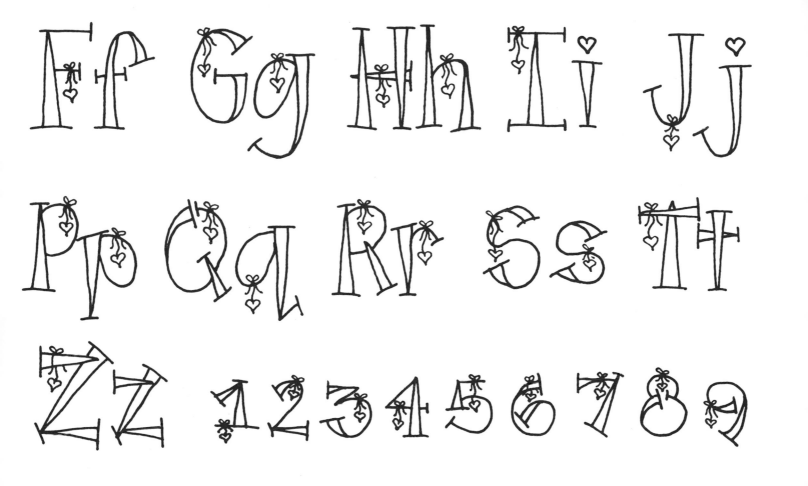

Aa Bb Cc Dd Ee

Kk Ll Mm Nn Oo

Uu Vv Ww Xx Yy

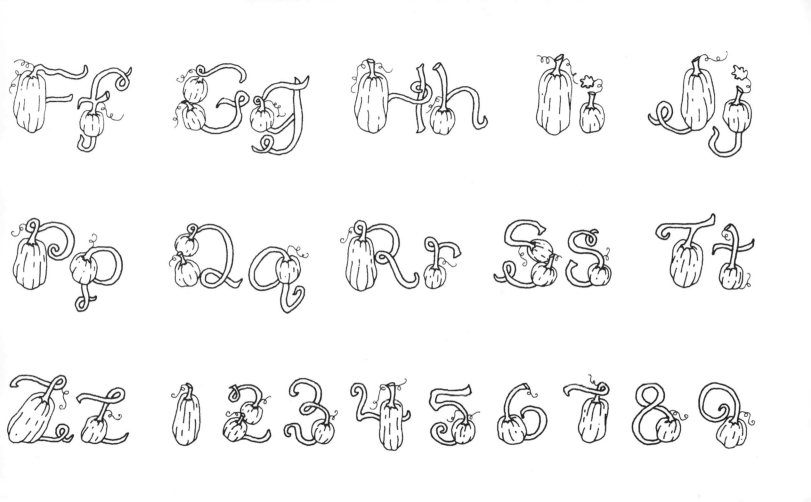

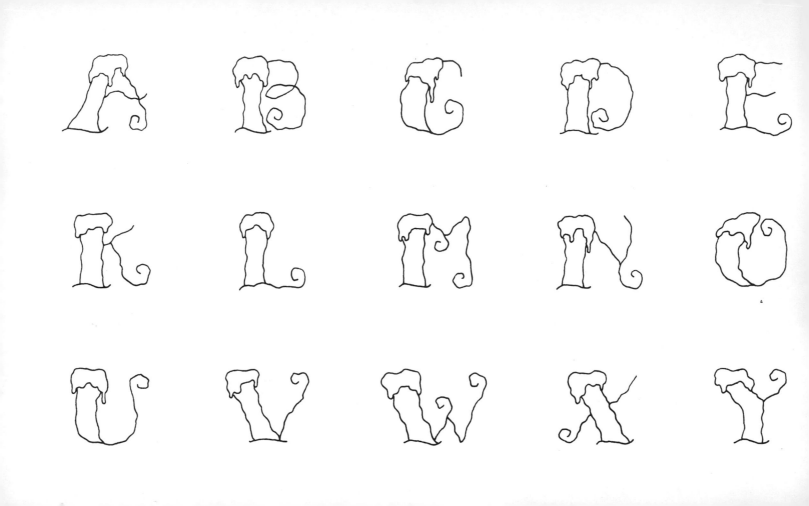

F G H I J

P Q R S T

Z 1 2 3 4 5 6 7 8 9

Send us your **incredible lettering** ideas. We'd love to see them!

Send your projects to:

Letter Art Editor

8400 Fairway Place

Middleton, Wisconsin 53562

Free catalogue!

Welcome to a world that's all yours—because it's filled with the things girls love! Beautiful dolls that capture your heart. Books that send your imagination soaring. And games and pastimes that make being a girl great!

For your free American Girl® catalogue, return this postcard, call 1-800-845-0005, or visit our Web site at americangirl.com.

Send me a catalogue:

	/ /
Name	Girl's birth date

Address

City	State	Zip

E-mail   *Fill in to receive updates and Web-exclusive offers.*

( )
Phone ❑ Home ❑ Work

Parent's signature   12583i

Send my friend a catalogue:

Name

Address

City	State	Zip	12591i

Try it risk-free!

American Girl® magazine is especially for girls 8 and up. Send for your preview issue today!

Mail this card to receive a risk-free preview issue and start your one-year subscription. For just $19.95, you'll receive 6 bimonthly issues in all! If you don't love it right away, just write "cancel" on the invoice and return it to us. The preview issue is yours to keep, free!

Send magazine to: (please print)

	/ /
Girl's name	Birth date

Address

City	State	Zip

Send bill to: (please print)

Adult's name

Address

City	State	Zip

Adult's signature

Guarantee: You may cancel at any time for a full refund. Allow 4–6 weeks for first issue. Non-U.S. subscriptions $26 U.S., prepaid only.

American Girl®

PO BOX 620497
MIDDLETON WI 53562-0497

Place
Stamp
Here